What We Were Born For

Poems by
Emilie Lygren

BLUE LIGHT PRESS ◆ 1ST WORLD PUBLISHING

1st WORLD
PUBLISHING

SAN FRANCISCO ◆ FAIRFIELD ◆ DELHI

Winner of the 2021 Blue Light Book Award

What We Were Born For

BLUE LIGHT PRESS
www.bluelightpress.com
bluelightpress@aol.com

1ST WORLD PUBLISHING
PO Box 2211
Fairfield, IA 52556
www.1stworldpublishing.com

BOOK & COVER DESIGN
Melanie Gendron
melaniegendron999@gmail.com

COVER ART
"Surfer" © Fiona Lee 2021
All rights reserved. www.thebrightagency.com

INTERIOR ART
"Seed Pod" by Hannah Teresa

AUTHOR PHOTO
Erika Lygren

FIRST EDITION

Library of Congress Cataloging-in-Publication Data

ISBN: 978-1-4218-3690-4

What We Were Born For

Table of Contents

Conditioning

Spring Hatch 1

The Coloring Book 2

A Deeper Pretending 3

Piano lessons 4

The Photographer 5

On the Impermanence of Tools 6

Photograph, Summer 2004 8

Weathering

Ritual 13

For the mother teaching her children to skip stones 14

A 10-year old finds a stick on a field trip to the beach 15

River, competence 17

Clutch 18

Meditation 19

Erosion 20

Revisioning

Blank is to Blank 23

For the students 24

What do you mean *nonbinary?* 26

The news 28

Birth cord 29

The Tyrant 31

For Michael Wayne Lively 32

Substitutions for Buttermilk 33

Make Believe 35

Birthday, shelter in place 36

Held 37

The sea spits back broken things 38

Apid 39

Italians Overheard 40

What my white elementary school teachers told me and my white classmates about Martin Luther King Jr., spoken (and unspoken) 41

On the evolution of shadows 43

Every time you pick up a knife, say "knife" 45

Next to the milk and sugar 46

You find hope when 47

For the grandmother teaching children how to plant seeds in the community garden 48

Acknowledgments 51

About the Author 52

Conditioning

Spring Hatch

One day at dusk the termites in unison exploded
from every wooded surface,
each stump and dead tree
marked by droves of soft-headed insects,
emerging into air
and making their first flights.
Some flew and fell to the ground,
wings in a tangle.
Others were snatched from midair
by a parade of evening birds,
juncos, tanagers, sapsuckers,
gathering food that would become
the wings of their own young.

As the termites floated through darkening skies,
I wondered how it felt to emerge from the tree stump,
to unfold those thinly webbed wings,
to crawl outside of darkness and the familiar
world of damp wood, to row through the air
with the movements of muscles unused.
And I wondered how I felt entering this life,
If after being washed and wiped dry and placed
into my mother's arms, those first few breaths
were anything like flight.

The Coloring Book

When I was five,
my babysitter gave me a coloring book.

Each day I was to fill in one page. Neatly.
She would place a gold star sticker
on each perfect drawing,
add a smiley face in green marker.
Slowly I worked through the book,
gold stars, gold stars.

One day I colored outside the lines.
Expanded the girl's striped shirt
with scribbles,
pretended it was windy,
drew the boy's hands alive
with extra arcs.

Later, she showed
me the book.

Large black X's through their bodies.
Frowns drawn over their smiles.
"No, no, no" written next to my inobedient lines.
No stars.

I cried,
I shuttered my wildness
when she closed the book.

A Deeper Pretending

Try to write a bad poem before breakfast.
    — *William Stafford, as quoted by Naomi Shihab Nye*

OK, I'll try,
but I have never been much good at being bad.

No, it's not like that!
It's not that I am good at everything,
or think I am.

It is a deeper pretending,
a tacit avoidance of things not yet known or learned,
a nodding along sometimes when people talk about that book
I should have read by now.

It started early.
"You're so quiet," they told me.
"So good at knowing things. So smart.
That's good!"

They told me so often it's all I thought I was.
Held up a trick mirror to show
only one edge of my humanity.

Why do we tell children they are anything?

I am still unraveling it,
the tight ball formed around
that one kernel of identity,

like today,
unsure of every word here,
catching myself thinking
I should get better at being bad
before doing it in front of anybody.

Piano lessons

Teach me everything there is to know about solemnity.
How to be grand,
full of circumstance.

To show you how serious
I am, how worthy,
I will never smile.

I too was tuned to
a scale of another's invention.

I think maybe we are the same.
The place you shine is inside —
strings, tightly wound,
humming
and wise.

The Photographer

Someday we will need to explain the
concept of a photographer:

(before phones), a person who carried a camera,
took the pictures
and rarely appeared in the frame.

There was forethought of film,
finding focus,
working with light.
There were days before development,
finite number of frames.

Growing up, the photographer was my mother.
In my mind I can still hear
the whirred flick of her Nikkormat,
the push of clickwheel to advance the film.

She brought me places.
She took photos and printed them out.
She told me
> People love talking about themselves,
> ask them questions.

When I look back at the photographs I can see what she saw.
Gift of time and perspective,
gift from the photographer.

> Oh Mom,
> The image I remember most is you,
> crouched down and holding the camera
> your long hair and small smile on the other side of the lens.

On the Impermanence of Tools

My dad raised me in a toolbox.
His answer to every question or trouble
was the right tool.

We softened our tough baseball gloves with oil.
We soaped car windows with massive sponges.
We painted over boredom with acrylic brushstrokes.
We pushed tomatoes through a sieve to catch the seeds.

As I grew older, he gave me my own tools —
a miniature watercolor kit,
a screwdriver and hammer when I moved out of the house,
a loved kitchen knife when I became a cook.

One day when I was inconsolably upset,
I went to my dad for help.
He didn't press me to tell him what was wrong,
he just handed me a trowel, smiled, and said

"Go outside. Dig a hole. You'll feel better."

I didn't know if I was supposed to bury my sadness
or if touching soft soil was meant to calm me,
but I did feel better.

Years later, I still dig holes when I am sad
and my dad still offers me
tools for my travels
but in the meantime
I have uncovered this truth —

that what I fear most is the day
I must dig a hole
for him,
when his tools will lose their warm hands.

There will be no hole I can dig large enough
to hold such sadness;
He will have left behind no tool with which
to cut through that grief.

Photograph, Summer 2004

My four teenaged best friends and I
ride down a river in inner tubes.
It is green summer everywhere.
I am closest to the camera,
raising my arms in attempted joy —

attempted, because when I rounded the bend
and saw my friend's mom holding the disposable camera,
I thought I had better look like I was having fun.

This is the silent pain of objectification,
the result of telling girls
they are pretty, or need to be,
asking them to smile.

Before long, you start to think you exist for others.

You live hovering a few feet away from the crown of your head,
looking back at yourself, assessing.

It is actually not much like living.

It is why I sought so much aloneness
in order to feel my own joy,
why it took me until twenty-nine
to learn to live
on the inside looking out.

It is why I take young women up steep mountains,
breath ragged.
Cells screaming for air.
No choice but embodiment.

We look at the horizon.
"This," we say, "This is what we were born for."

Weathering

Ritual

In each new place I look at the leaves.

Some are gray and withered, others gold or green.

The round spots of fungi, insect holes, split lines along veins all say:

I have been here long enough for here to change me.

May I stay half as long.

For the mother teaching her children to skip stones

Laughing, you skim flat, wide rocks across the river.

The stones sink,
stay,
will shape shift,
currents beyond your control
carving edges, wearing new forms.

You release them with a flick of your wrist,
stone,
stone,
stone.

So it is too with your children.

You shaped them,
sent them from your womb
in spasms of quick muscle.

You shaped them,
but the world will too.

You will not be the one to decide most of the time how it goes.

But you teach them anyway:
how to slow down and look,
how to crouch and
meet the flat mirror of water,
how to let go.

A 10-year old boy finds a stick on a field trip to the beach

"It reminds me of a
rabbit's ears!
No, a stretched out
letter z.
No, a crank handle
for an ice cream maker.
No, no wait it's a telephone!"

He talks fast
as he draws a picture of the
stick he found,
writes down everything
it reminds him of.

Then he holds the stick
above his head,
jumps up and down,
and watches the ocean
waves hiss over the
flat shoulders of the sand.

When it is time to leave,
he digs a hole
and buries the stick there.

After flattening the sand
he looks up at me and
proclaims,
"I'm going to come back
and find this stick again
and then I will feel exactly like I do now —
so happy."

As we walk away,
bouncing at my elbow,
he whispers,
"Do you think it will be the same,
when I come back?"

And I think about
about all the times I have
buried a part of myself
in hopes that I could come back
to find it unchanged, intact, whole —
tried to build a glass museum case
around a feeling that once sat in my ribcage,
or wove itself through my hair.

We look out across the bluffs.
A gull drops a feather,
and flies on.

River, competence

Rocks once ripped
from mountainsides,
broken branches of trees,
leaf or tuft of grass.

Swept up by
constant working currents,
blue undersides of streams,
mud unstuck from banks,
wed to clear movement.

Ripple pool and wave
reduce rough edges into roundness,
sand sticks into gleaming bare swords,
hold stones until their shapes converge.

Stay here long enough
and the parts of you, too,
that have been broken
will be made smooth.

Clutch

Where soil is swept away
or a tree tips over,
notice how the roots
still clutch rocks.
Touch the tangled arms
wrapped around boulders.
Feel how matter
shapes itself to stone.

Consider how we pick up
and mold ourselves to what is unyielding.
Notice what you were given to grow against,
the hard things you still grasp,
what you might hope to set down.

Meditation

Sitting near the window.
I watched a fly stammering
against the glass,
trying to break free
and transcend the
transparent boundary
it could not comprehend.

As I cupped my hands around the fly
then let it out the open door,
I wished that we could trade places —

that someone would gently remove me
from the invisible walls
I have pressed myself up against,
offer an opening I am too small to see.

After sitting longer,
I start to think that maybe I am all parts of the story —

the trembling fly,
the gently cupped hands,
the clear glass window,
the necessary air outside.

Erosion

Edges fall first,
silt grains cemented
under thousands of years
sloughed away by wind, rain,
footstep of dog,
sandstone alchemized beneath
weight of mountain
turns sand again

Subtle rubbing of days shapens us anew,
weathering, the
slowest song of change

No wonder we wake up some days
wondering at who we used to be.
No wonder we don't always notice
as our outer edges strip away.

No wonder the children build castles
made of sand at water's edge,
even though the castles fall.

They are practicing for
when they too will feel
what once seemed enduring
slip inside the rising tide.

Revisioning

Blank is to Blank

I dreaded the analogies section
during SAT practice tests in high school.
I failed every question.

ETERNAL : DURATION

harmonious : music
temporary : time
dry : water
omnipotent : power
weak : control

I could have made an argument for or against every one,
but there was no way
to tell the paper that.
Five choices.
One right answer.

The rows of
empty bubbles left my brain
penned in, flattened between boards.

Years have passed, and imagining
is still the most important thing
I ever learned to do.

For the Students

Sometimes we sit in circles with these questions:
>What are you afraid of?
>Who are your heroes and why?
>What do you do in your free time that really makes you
>free?

My students answer:
>*I have no free time. It is all full of homework, then I take care
>of my little sister.*
>*My hero is my brother because he walks me home so the bullies
>don't get me.*
>*Sometimes I am afraid my mother will work so hard she will
>die.*
>They are ten, maybe eleven.

I cannot follow them home
and fix it so their parents can
stop leaving,
take their books and burdens
for an hour a day
so they can go be children again.

>I can listen when they speak.
>I can turn their heads towards the sunrise,
>then to the dragonflies hatching by the creek.
>I can hold their packs while they run shouting
>towards an ocean they have never seen.
>I can dump the watering can on their heads
>on the hottest day of the year.
>I can honor their courage, and their joy.

I cannot always change the world they are living into,
but I can change the world we both live in
for the tremor of a moment,
the same way we all can for one other with a
small smile or knowing sigh
and the fierce act of living in the world with an open heart.

What do you mean *nonbinary?*

Sometimes I feel like wearing a dress
and letting my curls fall in neat-messy lines
and sometimes it only feels right to wear t-shirts,
buttoned flannel shirts,
tuck my hair into a soft beige cap.

Yes I am a woman
and I also often feel ungendered.

Not *between* as in the middle,
or going from one place to another
but *between* as its own country,
kaleidoscope of color
so much broader than the polarity
of pastel blue-and-pink baby bonnets.
Between as in the place of
        yes, and,
            ungendered, fluid,
until the world
shows me I appear female,
        says I am less deserving of professional attention,
        sweeps over me like dust under a rug,
        catcalls me and expects a smile.

I am not confused.
It is actually quite simple.
Joyful, even.
The more I live into it, the more clear I feel.

But my word processing program automatically corrected
ungendered to *endangered,*
and I still think about

the first-ever compliment a boy gave me,
I was in second grade,
it was the one day I wore a skirt all year,
brown corduroy with a purple and yellow-flowered shirt,
I had brushed my hair,
and as we waited to file into the classroom after recess he said
> *You look nice today, Emilie. At least, nicer than you did*
> *yesterday.*

And even then I found the comment
to be fantastically funny,
and the only confusing part was the empty replay of prescribed roles,
and somehow I knew not to be hurt,
knew I was so much bigger
even though I didn't yet have the words to say how.

The news

Each morning we listen for what is breaking —

the sound of a thousand tragedies fills the air,
shattering that never stops,
headlines, a fleet of anchors tangled at our feet.

We watch, worried
if we turn away even for an instant,
it will all crumble the rest of the way.

Forget with me for a moment.
Take an unguarded breath.
Do it now, the world needs your attention here, too,
on the rise and fall of your shoulders,
the rustle of leaves outside the window,
the warm space between your gaze and mine.

Birth cord

For Paul

The first thing children lose
is the feeling of floating —
absence of amnion,
first cradle, before gravity.

Then comes a snipped separation —
if it happens too fast,
we can forget our connection to everything.

If that continues we are left with a lonely man
pushing the once shining anvil of a wide land
off of a cliff.

We get birds looking at our radios thinking
"how difficult it is for them to just sing."

We yearn for the place where all the mothers
dead too soon
wish themselves alive,
try to phone their
children to say "I love you."
To say, "Look for places where you can still feel home."

We can't see it, but we can feel it in the afternoon,
floating dust and the smell of baked rock,
and an itch to return to water.

I ask,
"What do you remember about your mother?"

He replies,

"Right before dying, she said
'Turn on the tap so I can hear water running.
Open the window so for one last time, I can feel the air.'"

The Tyrant

Who knows the man behind the tyrant?

Did his father know him?
Or did he just know what he thought a son should be?

Did his mother know him?
Or was she an accomplice of the father?

Does his wife know him?
Or does she just know submission?

Do his supporters know him?
Or do they just see a mirror?

Do his children know him?
Or do they just know delusion?

Who knows the boy inside the tyrant?
Does anyone anymore?

He must be there somewhere.
I think he is probably alone, and afraid.

No one taught him how to fail,
how to make friends with anything but a clenched fist.

For Michael Wayne Lively

Before it was taken out of service and decontaminated, Michael Wayne Lively rode in the ambulance that had been used to ferry an Ebola-stricken patient to Dallas Presbyterian Hospital. The homeless drifter's subsequent disappearance spread fear throughout Dallas that a man at risk of Ebola was wandering the city.
– Dallas Newspaper, December 2014

You disappeared.

A city memorized your face, searched.
You were found, kept isolated
in a hospital room for 21 days,
fed, housed, clothed.
Once it was clear you weren't sick,
put back out on the streets.

I imagine you
facing the sliding glass doors,
possessions
in a plastic bag.
Maybe they gave you a juice box
or granola bar for the road —
to where, exactly?

If there was no space on the release form for finding out
if you had anywhere to go,
I like to think they would have asked anyway.

You disappeared again.
This time, no one said anything.

Substitutions for Buttermilk

Shelter in Place Day 16, Spring 2020

Find acid to induce curdling — lemon or vinegar
    so many things taste sour nowadays

Let sit for 15 minutes
    how quickly things can change

Is half and half a better approximate?
    I was only allowed one
    jug of milk at the store

Mixing butter and milk won't do it
    just another failure of language,
    like social distancing *or* camera phone

There wasn't any sugar in the store either
    they say it is like wartime almost,
    victory gardens again, can we do
    without with that much dignity?
    I feel hardly as brave.

Borrowing a cup from the neighbors seems risky
    never have we needed each other more

Maybe I will bake the cake next week
    will we learn anything
    from this practice of waiting?

Maybe it will be safe to go out again before the fires come
    nearby smoke, reason to stay inside,
    reason to prepare to leave quickly

Who has all the buttermilk, the sugar, the money
what are you saving it for?

When was toilet paper even invented?
we existed before it did,
and prison cells, and 2-day delivery, ATMs.

Didn't buttermilk come from what was leftover, anyway?
after this, after all this,
can we make something sweet
from what is left behind?

Make Believe

Mr. Rogers, what would you say to us now?
I miss your soft voice and slow smile.

Somehow you would remind us of what it means to share
        a neighborhood —
how our breath travels farther than we think,
but so can our care.

You would've made the puppets wear tiny cloth masks,
had them ask all the questions children need to ask like
        Why and *How long?* and *Can't we ...?*
let Daniel Tiger feel sad and angry, itchy under the ear straps.

You would have explained it all patiently and truthfully:
        No, we don't know how long.
        Yes, it's OK to feel afraid.
        This is how we care for everyone right now.

Maybe the adults would have listened, too.

Birthday, Shelter in Place

Dreams are different now,
there is not so much rushing.
Instead of tripping over
how or *when* or *how long*
I hold them gently
like a handful of helium balloons,
lie on my back
and examine them as
they float on long ribbons,
barely out of reach.

Today I can do nothing to bring them to ground.
There may be a slow release of air,
a settling, returns of some kind, or nothing.

So I watch as they twinkle in the sun,
delight in the bright colors and smooth corners,
notice where they move when the wind tugs,

notice how peaceful it is to pause
without trying to make anything come true.

Held

This was the summer
we ate almost all of the apricots ourselves.
Juice drip on chin and lip,
so many soft, sweet bites.

We picked them and wonder in-breathed
at red blush across tender velvet hemispheres,
skin how I imagine deer muzzles.

The ones we gave away,
we held our breath over,
a reverse sacrament,
placed them out to be taken and moved back.

    This was the summer we missed breathing into one another,
    missed neon apricot-colored shirts on the dance floor,
    missed the slick sweat of closeness without care,
    the summer we stutter-stepped and rearranged
    distant edges of invisible triangles
    as we passed one another by on
    the sidewalk and in the grocery store.

I wanted to rub you in apricots.
We unmasked and ate the fruit 10 feet away.

The sea spits back broken things

like softened glass,
hairless plastic doll.
Fragmented rim of once-proud porcelain plate.
Wood scrap reduced to smooth umber edge,
half a cinder block passes for a great, gray stone.

When the sea rises it will not give us back our lives, whole.

It will not give us back the voices of the islanders
or the cove where they fished for thousands of years.
Not the glaciers, already gone,
not the coastal cities built over centuries,
not the heat-stricken grandparents with no air conditioning.
Not the artists, or their murals, or the preschool chalk drawings
swallowed in floodwater.
Not the bleached white reefs once shimmered with fish,
the alpine trees and no higher ground.

There are no far-away lands when the largest forest burns.

When the last library is singed dry,
when it is too hot to grow tomatoes,
who will we be?
What pieces will fasten together our humanity then?

Apid

I saw 10 dead bees on my walk today–
10 small bodies lying on their sides or backs,
their wings still and smaller somehow.

How many flowers
did those soft faces push into?
How many pollen grains
staticked to the intricate forest of hairs on one leg?

Have you ever seen a bee up close —
(when it was alive, I mean)
look the next chance you get,
you will see its abdomen swell and contract
with breath, or blood, or maybe even something more holy.

Can you imagine summer without that faint buzz,
the background whisper:
> *We are here while you pause at the window sill*
> *or greet your children at the bus stop.*
> *While you bake cookies filled with finely chopped nuts,*
> *we speak the names of next year's seeds.*

This summer is long and rain has yet to come
and I found 10 dead bees on my walk today.
Take note, nothing is normal here.

Without them there might as well be no flowers —
take tweezers and try to cover half that ground.

When they stop, we stop.
When their wings fall,
We fall.

Italians Overheard

I heard her say
The Italian government gives 400 Lira a month
to people with celiac disease,
so they can buy medically safe food for themselves

and I wished to be from a country that
knows its limits, and accounts for them,
wished for a culture that clear,
one that hums along in daily greetings over the breakfast table

instead of begging to be asserted
over and over
through t-shirts and anthems,
through red hats and bluster,
through imperialism and exclusion,
fist fights,
ammunition,
unmasked individualism,
false freedom,
unrooted pride,
      all chanting
I am American, I am American, I am American, I am American

     (If we shout it enough times, maybe
     we will finally feel at home
     on the land we have stolen.)

What my white elementary school teachers told me and my white classmates about Dr. Martin Luther King Jr., spoken (and unspoken)

"*I Have a Dream* is the most important speech he ever gave."
      (we haven't listened to any others)

"His dream is real now."
      (race doesn't matter anymore)

"Everyone is equal now."
      (we don't see color)
      (we don't know our own history)
      (we don't know our own present)
      (don't worry, you're not racist)

"He believed in nonviolence,
which means being peaceful and calm."
      (we don't know our own history)
      (our history is confirmation bias)
      (we haven't read any more of Dr. King's writings)
      (or we don't want to tell you about them)

"We got here through nonviolence."
      (the trauma of racism does not count as violence)
      (the murders of black people at the hands of police do not count as violence)
      (poverty does not count as violence)
      (we don't know our own history)

"We did this together."
      (you can claim credit for what you have not done)
      (you are not a part of the problem)
      (there is no problem)
      (you are not racist)

"He was killed for speaking up for his beliefs, by someone who
did not want him to keep sharing them,
so now we honor and remember him."
>   (we don't want to think about how he was killed
>   by someone who looks like us)
>   (we don't want to remember how hated
>   he was in his lifetime)

"He was killed but his dream lives on."
>   (you are not racist)
>   (there is no more work to be done)

"You should remember to speak up for your dreams, too."
>   (talk even when you should listen)

On the evolution of shadows

Shadows swallow shadows,
stone shapes stone.
Everything argued into soft edgedness
by drip and drip of the rain,
the diligence of beetles.
Wonder– what was the first shape that
stepped in front of the sun,
left its imprint on the skin of the earth?
Was it a ridgeline thrust up from crust,
or rock cracked, darkness dropped from behind.
There was the infant moon's first eclipse,
trees turned into sundials,

wings sailed birds across the landscapes —
when did the beings of the ground learn

to fear what flew above?
Does the mouse dream of sleep
when the hawk
blocks the light?
Human hands arrived
and threw the ghost of
sparks on dim walls,
sent stone wheels rolling disks
of darkness over the ground.

We have made
a new library of outlines, wrought
webbing between stained glass,
straight-lined wooden benches,
teakettle, pencil, awl, airplane,
the space behind the picture frame,

each one also altered by entropy, borders fuzzed
through time.
But I want to beg the elements to fast forward
and wear through
machine guns,
prison wire,
police,
erode the sharpest
shadows, the hardest shadows,
the ones
I wish were only dreams.

"Every time you pick up a knife, say knife"

Kitchen Safety Manual

Know when you are holding something that could cause harm.
Say it out loud.
Say *hot, sharp, heavy*.
Say *rage, pride, pain*.

Say it, mostly to remind yourself.

Next to the milk and sugar

sit two cups for spoons
alongside each other, labeled:
Clean
Dirty

The spoons cycle between.

So forgiving we are with silverware,
so harsh with ourselves.

We think dirtiness is a state you stay in,
a smooth walled well
and no handles to climb out.
The long-ago mistake,
a smudge never to be scrubbed clean.

I will not stand for this.

I will not allow you
to think yourself

less malleable
than metal,
less deserving of cleansing,
of second chances.

You Find Hope When

You find hope when you remember that
your best friend was elected Prom Queen.

We were shocked.
She was not popular or plastic or a cheerleader,
like prom queens in the movies always were.

She was kind to everyone.

When things feel bleak, remember the people out there
who thought that mattered.

For the grandmother teaching children how to plant seeds in the community garden

"Just a little bit, they only
need to go down an inch,
make a small hole, use your pinkie,
put the seeds in,
gently, gently."

Elders pass on practice with invocation of earth under fingernails.
It doesn't matter so much if the rows are straight
so long as we remember ourselves.

We can spend a day like this, or a life,
let afternoons pass under
shifting light and swollen clouds.

Plants need no permission, only our exhale,
sunbeams, a thin veil of rain.

How many more hopeful acts do we have left?

After a thousand tragedies,
sleepless nights staring up at the rafters,
the ground beneath
is waiting to begin again,
the seeds will still be true.

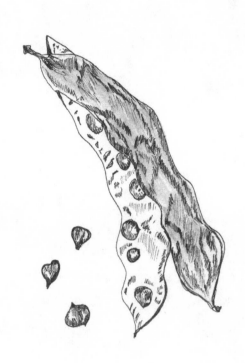

Acknowledgments

Earlier versions of these poems appeared in the following journals and anthologies:
Askew Poetry Journal,
The English Leadership Quarterly,
Index For The Next World,
New South,
Solo Novo,
Thimble Literary Magazine,
and *Watershed.*

About the Author

Emilie Lygren is a writer, outdoor educator, and facilitator who believes that poetry can change the world. She holds a Bachelor's degree in Geology-Biology from Brown University, and has over a decade of experience as a writer and as an outdoor science educator. Emilie has developed dozens of publications and curricula focused on outdoor science education and social-emotional learning through her work at the award-winning BEETLES Project at the Lawrence Hall of Science. She's also done stints as a kitchen manager, life coach, barista, mentor for teens, and event organizer. Emilie's poems have been published in *Thimble Literary Magazine*, *The English Leadership Quarterly*, and *Solo Novo*, among others. In writing and teaching, Emilie centers awareness and curiosity as tools to bring people into deeper relationship with themselves, their communities, and the places they inhabit. When she's not writing poetry, you'll likely find her somewhere on the Central Coast of California, talking to strangers, taking long walks, reading, or cooking for friends. Visit Emilie's website for more of her work and words: emilielygren.com.

CPSIA information can be obtained
at www.ICGtesting.com
Printed in the USA
LVHW111407250421
685504LV00017B/226

9 781421 836904